THE GREATEST JAPANESE PRISON ESCAPE: YOSHIE SHIRATORI

A Miso Soup Techinque

Shubham Vernekar
John Downey

S.M.V Publication

CONTENTS

ABOUT **YOSHIE SHIRATORI**

Prison breaks are mind-bending incidents. How is it possible that a prisoner could even dream about tooling together minimal supplies to make a bold dash for the exit door? Murderers, fraudsters, and all kinds of criminals have managed to flee their confined prison blocks, with some vanishing into thin air, never to be seen again, or at least never to be recognized again.

Yoshie Shiratori (July 31, 1907 - February 24, 1979) was born in July 31, 1907 in Aomori Prefecture, Japan. He is best known for having escaped from prison four times.

Yoshie Shiratori is Japan's own Harry Houdini, and not even handcuffs, copper walls, or a dislocated shoulder could stop his daring escapes. In Japanese Shiratori means swan.

Yoshie Shiratori was initially accused of murder and robbery and was sentenced to Aomori prison. In total he was sentenced to life plus 23 years that is 23 years more after his death, doesn't make any sense right. Later japan government has decided to free by looking at his efforts for the freedom and only served 26 years and was paroled in 1961. For his incredible escapes, Yoshie Shiratori became a legend, an **antihero in Japan**.Yoshie lived for another decade after that, doing odd jobs to survive. He eventually succumbed to a heart attack in 1979. His memorial is in the **Abashiri**

prison museum.

As horrendous as the experience must be for locals near prisons when rare escape attempts do work, it's impossible not to be enthralled by the daring, exciting nature of each burst for freedom. For all you simply can't condone a person's atrocious crimes or the escape itself, you sometimes have to respect the sheer ingenuity of some plots, while others are so farcical, it's impossible to believe they actually worked. Here is the most jaw-dropping, successful prison breaks in history of Japan...

CHAPTER 1 :
ESCAPE METHOD
=> LOCK PICKING.

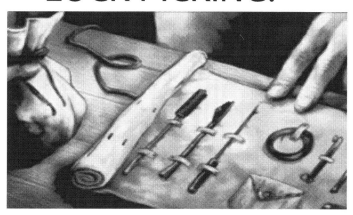

Aomori, Japan, 1936, prisoner Yoshie Shiratori had enough he was forced to confess to a murder he did not commit. Falsely imprisoned in Aomori Prison, where he was beaten and tortured every night by prison guards, and now worse, prosecutors were seeking the death penalty.

In his mind, it was time to go, but Aomori Prison wasn't the easiest to escape. Regardless, Yoshie Shiratori had nothing to lose. And so at 5:30 a.m. he made his move he knew there would be a 15 minute gap in the patrol time, as he had studied the **guard's**

routine for months. And when the coast was clear, he pulled out a **metal wire** which he had smuggled in from the bathhouse and started to pick the lock.

This was originally the metal support ring that was wrapped around the bathing buckets inmates use to wash themselves. His hands were stiff from the wintry cold but after a few minutes of picking, he had success, and his cell door swung open. But he wasn't out of the woods yet because there were more locked doors ahead.

He knew he only had a few minutes left before the guards would return, and so he wasted no time attempting to **pick** his way through the remaining **security doors**. Now fortunately for him he was able to make it out of the facility. But, the bad news was that he was only halfway to freedom. You see, he was still well within the search perimeter, which meant at any moment the alarm could go off and he'd still be caught.

At 5:45 a.m. the guards returned, peering into his cell and this is what they saw, Shiratori sound asleep in his futon bed. But of course, what they didn't realize was that they were looking at something else, a pile of loose floorboards underneath his duvet designed to trick them.

It wasn't until the next morning that they finally discovered the truth, and the alarm was sounded. But by then **Shiratori was long gone**. Now he had escaped.

But the things aren't always as they seem.

In fact, for Yoshie Shiratori, aka the Prison Break Magician, this was only the beginning.

To be continued in chapter 2.

CHAPTER 2 : LIZARD CLIMBER (CLIMBING COPPER SHEETS).

T hree days later he was caught trying to steal supplies from a hospital and just like that, he was back in the slammer.

But this time for his escape attempt he was sentenced to **life in prison**. He would never be with his family again - his wife and his daughter. And all the months of planning had led to just three days of freedom, and now it seemed he'd be locked up for a very long time.

Six years later, in 1942, in the midst of the Second World War, Shiratori found himself transferred to **Akita Prison** in Akita City.

There the guards treated him even worse than in Aomori they had heard about
Shiratori's previous escape and were determined to make an example out of him they wanted to make sure he would never escape again.

Along with the usual beatings, he was forced to partake in extreme manual labor, made to sleep on the hard concrete floor in the severe winter cold, and placed into **solitary confinement** for extended periods of time.

Now this was a specially-made solitary confinement cell which was very small and had a very high ceiling, with the walls covered with **copper sheets so smooth** that it was impossible to grip.

In addition, there was almost no sunlight even in the daytime, with the only window light coming from a small sealed skylight high above.

This was a room designed to keep escape artists from escaping. And if that wasn't enough, the guards also made sure that Shiratori was handcuffed at all times.

Now despite the constant abuse, one of the guards, **Kobayashi**, in fact the head
guard, took pity on him. Kobayashi never laid a finger, and even seemed to check up on him from time to time, concerned for his well being.

Perhaps this made life a little more bearable for Shiratori and it might have even been what kept his will alive all the way to the night of June 15th.

It was a stormy night, and Shiratori was in the middle of one of his extended stays in solitary confinement. At around midnight one of the guards peered into his cell and couldn't believe his eyes. He opened the cell door and looked around in astonishment, as Yoshie Shiratori had **vanished into thin air**.

All that was left was his handcuffs. **So how did he do it?** Well, there were a few assumptions the guards made that did not apply to Shiratori.

For one, handcuffs simply didn't work on him. Shiratori was actually a master
of getting out of handcuffs. And in fact, had several methods to choose from.

Here he decided to go with the familiar lock picking method. But he really could have gone with any of them. He had thoroughly scoured his surroundings to find anything that could be of use in an escape. And just like in Aomori Prison, he was able to uncover a loose bit of wire. Perhaps it was from one of the items Kobayashi brought him. But this wasn't clear.

After freeing himself from the cuffs, he placed his palms and soles of his feet on the smooth copper sheets and started climbing the unclimbable wall.

It turned out Shiratori was also an **expert climber** with an uncanny ability to scale like a lizard.

Once he reached the skylight above, he noticed that, yes, the window was sealed. But the wooden framing around it was starting to rot. And so thereafter night after night when the guards weren't looking, he climbed the copper walls and loosened the framing bit by bit.

Afterwards he'd climb back down and place the handcuffs back on as to not rouse suspicion.

After a couple of months, the window finally came loose. And from there it was just about choosing the right day.

He waited until a particular stormy night so the guards wouldn't hear the footsteps on the roof. And that was it. He had **escaped from prison again**. Now this time he wouldn't be caught.

Or at least, not in the way you'd expect.

Continued in Chapter 3

CHAPTER 3 : MISO SOUP TECHNIQUE.

T hree months later, on September 18th, the head guard, Kobayashi was at home when he heard a knock on the door.

To his surprise, it was the fugitive Yoshie Shiratori, **unkempt and disheveled**,
and he needed a favor. A stunned Kobayashi took him in and fed him, all the while listening to what he had to say.

Shiratori explained that he didn't actually mind being in prison and that the only reason he escaped twice now was due to the tremendous abuse he suffered at the hands of the sadistic guards.

Kobayashi, however, was the only one who treated him with any amount of respect. And so he felt he owed it to him to let him in on his **grand plan**.

Now this plan involved Shiratori willingly, yes, handing himself over to
the **Justice Department** where he could then personally make a case for how corrupt and barbaric the Japanese prison system was, and there needed to be reform.

He wanted to campaign for change, and in the process gain his legal freedom through a civil lawsuit. He felt this was the only way he could realistically
end up with **his family**.

This, of course, was a super ambitious plan. And as a fugitive on the run, he was well aware of that. Which is why he needed Kobayashi, the well-respected head guard of Akita Prison, to vouch for him to **strengthen his credibility**. As the only guard who ever treated him right, he had a feeling Kobayashi would do the right thing.

Minutes later, while Shiratori was in the toilet, **Kobayashi called the police**.

Maybe not a great plan. Just like that, Shiratori was back in prison, and this time he vowed never to trust an officer of the law again.

For the second escape, the courthouse added three more years to his life sentence. Now Shiratori requested to be sent to a **Tokyo prison** where the weather was warmer, as he couldn't stand the cold in the northern prisons.

His previous stints had weakened him severely, but he was denied his request. Instead the judge sentenced him to the infamous **Abashiri Prison** in Hokkaido,
the northernmost prison in Japan.

No man had ever escaped from this wintry hellhole of a prison. It was now 1943, and the cold was unbearable in Abashiri as the temperature in the cells was **below freezing point**.

Whenever inmates received their prison food, the **miso soup** and soy sauce would often freeze up.

In this temperature a handcuffed Shiratori was thrown into an open cell in summer clothing, and he immediately felt the **paralyzing** sting of cold air.

Perhaps in a fit of desperation, he tried to force himself past the guards. But they were able to push him back and **beat him** down. An enraged and defiant
Shiratori stood back up and **vowed** that he would escape from Abashiri Prison, like he's always done, and that there was nothing they could do about it.

In fact, he claimed there was little point even putting handcuffs on him, as he'd always find a way to break free, if not by lock picking, then well, this.

He the proceeded to rip apart the chain of his handcuffs to the horror of the guards. It turned out Shiratori had another special ability. Aside from his outstanding climbing abilities, he also possessed **incredible strength**, almost **superhuman strength**.

Back in Akita Prison he could have broken free of the cuffs the physical way if he didn't have to put them back on. Now this was impressive, but it wasn't so smart to lay his cards on the table like that, as the guards were starting to
build an escape profile on him.

They knew he had lock picking abilities, lizard-like climbing abilities, and now almost superhuman strength. And so they set out to devise the ultimate escape-proof cell, one that was sure to be **Shiratori proof**.

And they came up with this. The new cell had steel fixtures with a low chance of rot. Any openings, even the bars removed, were made **smaller than his body**, meaning there was no way he could physically fit through.

He had specially made solid iron handcuffs that tied his hands behind his back, and leg cuffs that made him barely able to stand.

These **cuffs weighed 20 kgs** each and had no keyhole, which meant they could not be lock picked. And the only way they could be removed was by two metalwork specialists who would come once every **few weeks to remove** them in an arduous two hour process.

It was at this point, and only this point, that he could even take a bath. And he certainly needed one as weeks of being shackled up with no movement meant his cuff wounds were infested with maggots.

On top of that, and as cold as it had already been, it wasn't even peak winter yet.
Any strength he would have left would surely be **nullified** by the upcoming freeze.

Though just in case, they still made sure to cut his already **meager food portions** in half.

And so that was it.

Even for Shiratori, this was too much. As winter came he succumbed to his fate.   Every day the guards would slide his meal through the opening and he'd be forced to grovel **like a dog**.

His hand and leg cuffs made every action awkward and uncomfortable, with
even sleeping being a **pain**.

There was no doubt life in Abashiri Prison was **absolute torture**.

Now fast forward.

Shiratori was somehow able to survive through the winter, and spring was coming. This meant he was starting to get his strength back.

But still, what could he really do? He was literally in a bind.

Months passed and well, nothing seemed to happen. Then **one night** in August,
a guard in his office was doing some paperwork when he heard some shuffling on the roof.

He wasn't sure what it was, but he decided to check on the prisoners. As he looked inside Shiratori's inescapable cell, **he was stunned**.

The futon bed and prison garments were neatly folded up. The specially made 20 kg handcuffs and leg cuffs that would have required two specialists two hours to remove was placed on the side.

And Shiratori was **nowhere to be seen**.

He had finally fulfilled his promise to the guards. The alarm immediately sounded, but despite the work of the search party, it seemed he had **truly disappeared**.

But how on earth did this happen?

How did he escape from the fortress that was Abashiri Prison? Well, preparation had started six months earlier. At the time he didn't have the strength or stamina to mount any sort of escape, not to mention the restraints he was in.

The one thing he did have was **time and patience**. Every day the guards would slide his meal through. And while he struggled to eat his food off the floor, he always made sure to save a little bit of the miso soup in the corner.

You see, every night he would hobble awkwardly to the inspection window and splash a little of it on the steel frame. He would also dab some on his handcuffs and leg cuffs.

Now his intention was for the **salt content** of the miso soup to oxidize the screws and bolts, eventually corroding and loosening it. After a month, this technique of **rusting** through the iron actually worked, and the first screw came out.

The next few months saw screws and bolts coming loose assisted by the use of the first screw as a sort of screwdriver.

By the end of spring, he was able to fully remove his handcuffs and leg cuffs, as well as the steel frame of the inspection window.

But there was a problem. The size of the opening was smaller than his body, which meant he couldn't fit through, a contingency thought out by the guards.

What they didn't account for though was **Shiratori's fourth ability**, which involved being able to **dislocate his joints at will**.

With this he was now able to slide through the opening like a **caterpillar**. This repertoire of skills thus surely making him an honorary member of the X-Men.

With that he climbed through a broken window in the roof and vanished.

Impressively, Shiratori had now escaped from three prisons, as well as being the **only man to ever escape Abashiri Prison**.

Continued in Chapter 4

CHAPTER 4 : DIGGING THE FLOOR.

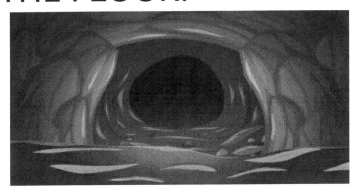

N ow good on him for escaping, but this was northern Hokkaido. And the only direction he could have gone to was the cold, snowy mountains.

Actually, the prison guards felt that they had the last laugh because if the cold didn't get him the mountain bears certainly would. Despite this likelihood,
there was one person who stayed hopeful, and that was **Shiratori's wife.**

But she was still worried. Because even if he was alive, she knew he wouldn't be able to make it back to his family as the authorities would be constantly on his tail.

Which is why she was desperately and secretly hoping that Japan would lose the war, as that would enable the **US** to take over the country, meaning everyone would likely forget about her husband.

Of course, she kept this to herself. But then a year later, in August 1945, she got her wish.

bombs exploding

The Americans had now taken over the country's penitentiary system, and
sweeping changes were being made. And it did seem perhaps that the manhunt for Yoshie Shiratori had now taken a back seat.

Yet the question remained, where was he, and **was he even alive?**

The answer was yes, he was alive and living a solitary life, this time self-imposed.

It turned out he had discovered an abandoned mine on a mountainside in the Hokkaido wilderness and was able to make a home for himself.

For food he lived off nuts and berries, wild rabbits and raccoons, and was even able to learn to catch crabs from a stream by observing the **habits of bears**.

Life was steady and safe. But after a while, curiosity got the better of him. And so after **two years of isolation** he made his way down the mountain to a nearby village.

What he saw astounded him. The streets were filled with signs written in English.

The posters and flags emblematic of the war effort had vanished. And even more strange, young Japanese girls were holding hands with **American soldiers**.

What on earth was going on?

He grabbed a newspaper that had been set aside, flipped through the pages, and it was only then that he found out about the atomic bombs, Hiroshima and Nagasaki. Japan had surrendered the previous year, and he couldn't believe it.

As with his wife, he felt it was now pointless to hide. And so bid farewell to his
old hunter-gatherer lifestyle.

He headed south of Abashiri for the next 50 days until he reached the city of Sapporo.

At this point he was starving. So he found himself a nice **ripe to-mato** from a nearby field, which was a huge mistake.

A **farmer** had spotted him and mistook him for a well-known local thief, which led to a scuffle resulting in the farmer's abdomen being pierced by a blade.

Sadly he bled out and **died**. But not before Shiratori was arrested for the crime.

It wasn't long until police found out that they had in fact had the infamous Yoshie Shiratori in their custody.

For his multiple escapes and having now murdered the farmer, despite his claims of self-defense he was sentenced to death by the **District Court of Sapporo**.

And in 1947, he was sent to **Sapporo Prison** to await execution. Now to ensure he wouldn't escape this time while on death row, he was placed under 24 hour surveillance with six armed guards personally assigned to his watch.

As for the cell itself, it was upgraded further from the one in Abashiri Prison with **reinforced** doors, ceilings, bars, windows.

In fact, any openings were made smaller than the size of his head, not just his body, learning from the Abashiri escape.

As while he may be able to dislocate his joints, he certainly can't dislocate his skull. As long as his head can't fit, they were good.

The six guards were so confident in fact that they didn't even bother cuffing him. Now Shiratori was **getting old** and the odds of escaping by this point were looking slim.

As his execution loomed near, there was little he could really do, and the guards knew that.

They could see the desperation on his face, looking up, searching for an escape plan that they knew would never come. Though still, just in case, they made sure to **search his room** every night while he was taking a bath in the bathhouse, inspecting the ceiling, skylight, and any other openings.

A month passed and winter was now coming, weakening him further. And the realization was starting to dawn on him.

He grew increasingly despondent, staying in bed, refusing to wake up **despite the orders** of the guards. This went on for a while, until one morning, the guards had enough and entered the cell to discipline him.

They flipped over the duvet and **he was gone**. This was not possible.

How did he do it this time?

Going back to when he was first placed under 24 hour surveillance with the six armed guards personally assigned to his watch.

He had in fact conditioned them to look up and keep up from the very start, not just because his previous escape attempts involved climbing through skylight windows on ceilings, but also his suspicious, yet as it turned out very intentional, behavior of constantly looking up to figure out an escape plan.

Little did they know, it was **all an act** and that he already had one. But it would be taking place precisely where they weren't looking.

You see, it turned out the authorities were so concerned with him escaping through a window or skylight that they neglected to **reinforce the bottom**.

This ironically ended up being his easiest and simplest escape because all he had to do was remove the bolted floorboards, which wasn't easy but he had experience, and using random cutlery and a miso soup bowl, **dig his way** to freedom.

This took over a month. And he was able to hide his activities due to
1st: the guards not suspecting this approach, and
2nd: the floorboard panels being put back in place every night after digging.

The six guards thought they were keeping a good eye on him even at night. But with the hole consistently positioned underneath the futon and duvet and it increasingly becoming the norm to refuse the orders of the guards to wake up, nothing seemed out of the ordinary.

Placing a pile of loose floorboards underneath the duvet to trick them was also a callback to his first prison escape in Aomori.

So he had now escaped from prison four times.

Continued in chapter 5

CHAPTER 5 : THE FINAL FREEDOM.

B y this point the story is starting to get ridiculous. But this perpetual cycle of capture and escape, capture and escape, was about to end. Because a year later, in 1948, Shiratori was exhausted. He was in his 40s now. And this was a young man's game.

One day in the **Kotoni neighborhood**, still in Sapporo, as he stopped to rest, a policeman just happened to sit by his side for a **smoke**.

He didn't know who Shiratori was, but he struck up a conversation with him. Shiratori, of course, was wary of his presence and tried to play it cool, all the while attempting to figure out a way to remove himself from the situation **without being suspicious**.

Suddenly the policeman did something unexpected, at least to him. He pulled out another cigarette and **offered it to him**.

Shiratori was stunned. You see, cigarettes were expensive luxury items in Japan at the time. And the fact that someone offered it to him just out of the **kindness of his heart** brought tears to his eyes.

Not to mention all his life he had been abused and mistreated by officers of the law, with even the head guard, Kobayashi, turning his back on him. And here was an instance of an officer treating him kindly with respect, and with **no prejudgment**.

As he smoked the cigarette, Shiratori **couldn't help** but tell the officer his full name, Yoshie Shiratori, and that he had escaped from Sapporo Prison last year.

In fact, he had escaped from prison four times in his life. It was strangely a relief to get it all off his chest, and he was even ready for the consequences.

After the Kobayashi incident he had vowed never to trust another officer of the law again. But the simple act of receiving a cigarette from a **stranger broke him**.

Of course, **he was arrested again**, but this time things were different.

Maybe it was the fact that he willingly gave himself up, or that Japan's justice system was going through a change. But the High Court of Sapporo
became sympathetic to Shiratori's plight. And some of his past claims were recognized, such as acknowledging the farmer's death as a legitimate case of **self defense**.

They also made note that throughout all four of his prison escapes he didn't kill or injure a single guard, despite the abuse he may have suffered at the ends.

At the end of the deliberation, the High Court dismissed the murder charge, **revoking his death sentence**, and instead sentenced him to just 20 years in prison.

Further, they approved his request to be transferred to a Tokyo prison where the weather was warmer. He was getting what he wanted.

In **Tokyo** he was sent to **Fuchu Prison** where, for the first time, the guards actually **treated him well**. It was a weird feeling.

There were all these precautions and security measures in place to ensure that the infamous Prison Break Magician wouldn't escape. But the truth was Shiratori didn't really care anymore.

Everything he'd been fighting against, the mistreatment from guards, the death penalty, even the northern climate, was no longer of concern.

And he was at peace.

There was no need to escape anymore. He finally accepted his punishment. And for the remainder of his sentence acted as a model prisoner.

Just **14 years later**, in 1961, he was released on parole. And for the first time in a long time he was **truly a free man**.

He decided to head back to **Aomori** where it all began and meet up with his **daughter**, who by this point unfortunately was the only family member he had left.

For his incredible escapes, Yoshie Shiratori became a legend, an **antihero in Japan**. But it was very much the opposite for the country's penitentiary system, which had somehow allowed him to escape time and time again.

This was a national embarrassment for Japan.

But just as preventing criminals from breaking out of the system is vital for the safety of society, so is preventing them from breaking into the system.

Yoshie lived for another decade after that, doing odd jobs to survive. He eventually succumbed to a heart attack in 1979.

AFTERWORD

Thank You for being the part of this inspiring man story, hope you like it. Yoshie Shiratori has fight against all his odds and never give up, this story teaches us to never give up in life and hope for the best in life.

Lot more books are comming in future to get update's about our latest books follow my author page on amazon
https://www.amazon.com/author/smv
Also follow our facebook page
https://www.facebook.com/SMV-Publication-101792704860707/

Thank You.

Printed in Great Britain
by Amazon